PAROCHIAL PROBLEMS

A Play

MARGARET WOOD

SAMUEL **FRENCH**

LONDON
NEW YORK TORONTO SYDNEY HOLLYWOOD

CHARACTERS

Mrs Preece, housewife
Mr Griffiths, churchwarden and secretary to the P.C.C.
Owen Pugh, Mr Meredith's labourer
Morgan Meredith, builder and decorator
Miss Jones, schoolmistress
Mrs Evans, a formidable housewife
The Vicar
Gareth

The action takes place in the Parish Hall at Bowen's Cross

Time—the present

Please note our NEW ADDRESS:

Samuel French Ltd
52 Fitzroy Street London W1P 6JR
Tel: 01 - 387 9373

PAROCHIAL PROBLEMS

The Parish Hall at Bowen's Cross. Afternoon

Mrs Preece, a housewife, is putting out paper and pencils on the long baize-covered table which runs at an angle across one side of the stage with chairs round it. Behind the table is a door. On the opposite side of the Hall is a second door, with a window downstage. The usual notices and board are displayed. Below the window is a small table with a carafe of water and a glass. Mr Griffiths is standing by the window, staring gloomily out. He is the Churchwarden and Secretary to the P.C.C. There is a moment's pause, while Mrs Preece deals out papers emphatically

Mrs Preece (*over her shoulder to Griffiths*) We shall need the water for the Vicar, Mr Griffiths.

Griffiths (*without turning*) What for? He never touches a drop—even though it *is* only water.

Mrs Preece Never mind. (*Tapping the centre of the table where the Vicar is to sit*) Put it in front of him. It shows who's in charge of the meeting.

Griffiths (*bringing it, grudgingly*) Needs something to show it, doesn't it? He couldn't keep a Sunday School in order, let alone a Parochial Church Council meeting. (*He dumps the water on the table*)

Mrs Preece (*counting agenda papers round the table*) Mrs Evans, Mr Griffiths, the Vicar, me, Mr Meredith—still, he's improving things, isn't he? Miss Jones, Mr Prosser and Mr Williams. (*The last two are placed on the table on the side nearest the audience, as the people concerned never appear*)

Griffiths (*returning to the window and looking out*). Improving? What things? Where *is* everybody?

Mrs Preece He got Lloyd the post office off the P.C.C. That's one less thorn in the flesh.

Griffiths And put Mrs Gwynn Evans on. That's one more.

Mrs Preece Well, you can't say he isn't improving the church. Lovely white walls and blue paint. Better than that old yellow distemper that's been flaking off on the faithful for the last thirty years.

Griffiths Yes, I must say that Morgan Meredith is making a nice job of it; even though he's only got half-baked Owen Pugh to help him.

Mrs Preece (*moving towards the window*) And there's Owen coming across the churchyard now; leap-frogging over his own grandfather's headstone and landing on Jones the Black Bull, R.I.P.

Griffiths They'd take the strap to him if they knew who was taking liberties with their private property.

Mrs Preece You can't blame Owen, poor lad. He's not got all his chairs at home.

Griffiths So they say. It's my impression that Owen does very nicely out of being simple-minded. (*He moves to the table*).

Owen enters by the door above the window, whistling cheerfully. He is the attractive type of simpleton, with childish ambitions and enthusiasm—not an oaf

Owen (*sunnily*) Oh, hallo, Mrs Preece. Hallo, Mr Griffiths.

Griffiths You can't come in here now, Owen. This is a P.C.C. meeting.

Owen (*looking round*) A very small meeting, Mr Griffiths.

Griffiths It's going to be larger, you stupid boy. They haven't all come yet. (*He sits*).

Owen I was looking for Mr Meredith, see.

Mrs Preece (*from the window, where she is watching for arrivals*) Can I give him a message?

Owen I want to know what to do next. I've finished the job I'm on, see.

Griffiths And what was that?

Owen Painting round the back of the organ. Mr Meredith thought I'd be all right there, because if I made a mess of it, only the boy that pumps the organ would see it.

Griffiths And have you made a mess of it?

Owen (*beaming*) No, Mr Griffiths. Nice job I've done, considering.

Griffiths Considering what?

Owen (*sheepishly*) Considering I don't often make a nice job of anything.

Mrs Preece (*kindly*) Don't you underrate yourself, Owen. I'm sure you're learning fast.

Owen (*eagerly*) Oh, yes, Mrs Preece. I am. Mr Meredith says p'raps he'll let me go up the scaffolding before we've finished.

Mrs Preece What? Right up to the ceiling of the church?

Owen If I go on as I'm doing at present, he says. (*Rapt*) Halfway to heaven that'd be for me, Mrs Preece, up there with the cherubs on the ceiling.

Griffiths And half way to the other place if you fall off on the way up. I hope Meredith's got you insured. As for those cherubs, you'd better take a good look at them, because you'll be painting them out before the end of the week. Good thing too. Ugly, badly-painted, sentimental daubs.

Mrs Preece Ah, ah! Here's Mr Meredith coming now.

Meredith enters from the door above the window. He is middle-aged, humorous, but cunning

Meredith Afternoon, Mrs Preece. Afternoon, Mr Griffiths. Ah— Owen. Done that bit of wall, boy?

Owen Looks a treat, Mr Meredith. Pity no one can see it but the blower boy.

Meredith Well, now I'll give *you* a treat.

Owen (*eagerly*) The scaffolding?

Meredith (*impatiently*) No, no, no. You go and start painting the front porch door. Everybody will see that.

Owen (*deflated*) Yes, Mr Meredith. (*He starts to go*)

Meredith Owen.

Owen turns

Get the ladder, start at the top and work down.

Owen Yes, Mr Meredith. (*He goes to the door above the window*)

Meredith Owen.

Owen turns

Undercoat first; then gloss.

Owen Yes, Mr Meredith.

He goes through the door

Meredith (*shouting*) And Owen. . . .

Owen's face reappears

Put the paint pot where you won't step back into it.
Owen (*meekly*) Yes, Mr Meredith.

Owen disappears

Meredith He went back home with odd feet last week—one white emulsion and one blue gloss. (*Picking up the agenda*) What have we on the menu this time? Redecoration of the church; date of Mothers' Union Outing; date of Sunday School Outing, (*He sits*) Crammed with excitement as usual.
Griffiths With Mrs Evans on the committee it might be just that. She was absent last time—and so were you. Nice and peaceful. We got a lot done. (*Fretfully, looking at watch*) It's just on time. Vicar ought to be here. (*He goes to the window*)
Mrs Preece He'll be across at the school, hearing the children their catechism or something. Wasting their time and Miss Jones's.
Meredith I agree. He's round there far too much. Parsons ought not to be bachelors. They're a walking temptation to every unmarried woman in the neighbourhood. It's the dog collar that does it.
Mrs Preece (*archly*) What about eligible widowers, Mr Meredith? Aren't they walking temptations too?
Meredith (*shortly*) You mind your own business, Olwen Preece.
Mrs Preece Ooh! There now! (*With meaning coyness*) A very nice woman, Miss Jones. Don't know why she wasn't married years ago.
Meredith (*irritably*) What's he think he's doing, keeping her all this while? Half-past three she's supposed to finish.
Griffiths (*turning*) Here she comes now.
Meredith About time. She's done half an hour's overtime for no pay.

Miss Jones enters, a neat pleasant woman of about thirty

Meredith rises, smiling, and pulls out her chair for her

Miss Jones I'm sorry I'm late, the Vicar kept me. Oh, thank you, Mr Meredith. (*She sits*).

Griffiths Where *is* the vicar? If you can be here, so can he.

Miss Jones Mrs Morgan caught him at the gate. She's already complained to me because she doesn't want her Megan to sit next to Dylan Price. Says he smells.

Meredith Fair play, he does. All the Prices smell. If you run a broiler house and process the droppings, it stands to reason, doesn't it? What did you do, Miss Jones?

Miss Jones I told her Dylan's mother had already asked me to move Megan because she sniffed all the time. We parted honours even, I think.

Meredith Ah, you're a smart girl, Miss Jones, and no mistake.

Griffiths (*returning to the table*) Mrs Evans is advancing up the path.

Meredith Attention all shipping! Here is a gale warning.

Miss Jones (*laughing*) Oh, Mr Meredith! You mind you're not wrecked in the storm.

Mrs Evans enters, a dominating, permanently indignant woman

Various persons (*sweetly*) Good afternoon, Mrs Evans.

Mrs Evans Good afternoon. (*Looking round*) And where is the Vicar, I'd like to know?

Griffiths We'd all like to know.

Miss Jones Not like you to be late, Mrs Evans. Not that you are, since the meeting's not begun.

Mrs Evans Circumstances beyond my control. Not that any of you would be interested in *that*!

Meredith On the contrary, Mrs Evans, anything beyond your control must be worth hearing about.

Mrs Preece What happened?

Mrs Evans Last night Gareth Pugh's rotten elm tree came down right across our pump house. Stopped the pump.

Mrs Preece What—the one that pumps up water for the whole village?

Mrs Evans There's no other pump, is there? And were any of you short of water this morning?

Griffiths Not that I noticed.

Mrs Evans And are you grateful?

Griffiths (*fretfully*) You tell us what we're to be grateful for and we'll try to oblige.

Mrs Evans From five a.m. this morning Mr Evans and I have been chopping and sawing and clearing that branch so as he could get to the pump. Which he did; all for you. And you asleep in your beds at the time.

Mrs Preece Well there, now. It's grateful we are indeed, Mrs Evans.

The Vicar enters, flustered and nervous

Vicar Good afternoon, everybody. You're very punctual.

Mrs Evans No we're not. You're late.

Vicar Oh dear. Am I really? Well, we must get on, then, mustn't we? (*He sits*).

Griffiths (*banging down two letters in front of him*) Apologies for absence.

Vicar Oh—thank you. This one—(*he hastily scans it*)—is from Mr Prosser, who regrets that he cannot be here owing to a previous engagement—(*picking up the other*)—one from Mr Williams—saying much the same thing.

Meredith Ah. Chepstow Races.

Vicar Well, there seem to be no more apologies . . .

Griffiths No more absentees, are there?

Vicar Eh?

Griffiths We're all here except those two.

Vicar So we are, so we are. Then I call upon Mr Griffiths to read the minutes of the last meeting.

Griffiths (*rising*) Minutes of the meeting of the Parochial Church Council held in Bowen's Cross Parish Room on February twenty-second last. Present were Miss Jones, Mrs Preece, Mr Williams, Mr Preece, Mr Griffiths. Apologies were received from Mrs Evans, Mr Meredith. The minutes of the previous meeting having been read, confirmed and signed, the committee proceeded to a discussion of the redecoration of the church.

Owen bursts in excitedly

Owen It's finished, Vicar, it's finished!

Vicar (*irritably*) What's finished? You can't come in here . . .

Owen The big thermometer! The one that's to stand outside the church to take the temperature of the Restoration Fund. Gareth has just brought it up on his lorry. Can we bring it in?

Vicar No, you can't. We're having a meeting. I . . .

Meredith (*rising*) We ought to see it, you know, Vicar. If Owen and his pals have made it, anything might be wrong.

Vicar Oh, very well. Bring it in, Owen, bring it in . . .

Owen goes out delightedly and Gareth and he stagger in with a large hardboard cut-out thermometer, marked from the bottom in hundreds with heavy cross lines for the thousands. It goes up to at least £6,000. They rear it up against the back wall and stand grinning proudly, one each side

Meredith (*strolling up to it*) Not bad, Owen. Not bad at all.

Owen See those little pointers that slide up and down to show how we're doing? *I* made those. How much money have we got to raise, Mr Griffiths?

Griffiths (*going to look*) The target is two thousand five hundred, Owen. So you put the top pointer there.

Owen slides up the top pointer

Owen And how much have we got already, sir?

Miss Jones comes to inspect the thermometer

Griffiths Including last Sunday's collection and the Flower Club's exhibition, four hundred and fifty-eight pounds, twenty-five pence. (*He slides the other pointer right down and returns sourly to his place*)

Owen Diawl! That's an awful long way to climb, Mr Griffiths.

Miss Jones You've done it very nicely, boys. All the numbers in the right order, too.

Owen Oh, Gareth did the numbers. He could count to a thousand when he was only a mixed infant.

Miss Jones Very good, Gareth. You were always a neat worker.

Gareth (*grinning with pleasure and embarrassment*) Thank you, Miss . . .

Vicar And thank *you*, boys. It's quite splendid, quite splendid. Now, we must get on with the meeting.

Gareth touches his cap and goes

Owen lingers, lovingly fingering the pointers

Meredith Back to work, Owen.

Owen goes

Vicar Now, Mr Griffiths, we'll proceed.

Miss Jones and Meredith sit

Griffiths H'm, h'm . . . (*He finds his place*) The minutes of the previous meeting having been read, confirmed and signed, the committee proceeded to a discussion of the redecoration of the church. It was finally agreed unanimously that it should be repainted throughout in white, with the woodwork in deep blue.

Mrs Evans That is not correct, Mr Chairman.

Griffiths (*drawing himself up*) Are you saying that I am a liar, Mrs Evans?

Mrs Evans I don't know yet. P'raps you just can't write minutes.

Griffiths Mrs Evans, I have written minutes, man and boy, ever since . . .

Mrs Evans Then it's about time you wrote them accurately.

Vicar (*trying to pour oil on troubled waters*) What exactly are you referring to, Mrs Evans? Though really we should discuss this after I have asked whether you approve the minutes as correct.

Mrs Evans I've told you. They aren't.

Griffiths What's incorrect about them?

Mrs Evans You said it was *unanimously* agreed that the church should be redecorated throughout.

Griffiths You were not present, Mrs Evans, so I fail to see . . .

Mrs Evans I was not present owing to a funeral at Bargoed which I had to attend, it being my last surviving uncle. But my neighbour Mr Williams was here, wasn't he? So I know it wasn't a unanimous vote. He voted against it.

Miss Jones (*waking up*) That's right. He did. I remember because I was a bit undecided myself.

Mrs Evans But you didn't speak up, did you?

Miss Jones I told you—I was undecided . . .

Vicar Mrs Evans, *please*! We must not let things get out of hand.

I think it is the word "unanimous" that is at fault, Mr Griffiths.

Griffiths If we had a bit of order at these meetings, I might be able to tell whether something was unanimous or not.

Vicar Yes—well—perhaps you should delete the word unanimous and substitute that after discussion it was agreed by a vote of— (*he rapidly assesses the number*)—five-to-one that the church should be redecorated throughout.

Griffiths stoops to make the amendment

Mrs Evans (*folding her arms complacently*) You can spare yourself the trouble, Mr Griffiths, because you've still not got it right.

Griffiths (*slamming down his pen*) Vicar! You are the chairman and I expect you to act as such. (*He sits, enraged*).

Vicar (*rising*) I really think, Mrs Evans, that we must allow Mr Griffiths to finish reading the minutes. After that we can go on to matters arising.

Mrs Evans This isn't matters arising. It's matters that should never have arisen. There's two lies in Mr Griffiths's minutes . . .

Griffiths (*springing to his feet*) Slander, Mrs Evans, I know what I'm talking about: nobody will call me a liar and get away with it!

Mrs Evans Prove it, then. Read your minutes and I'll have you and the Vicar in court for falsifying the record for your own ends!

There is a general reaction

Vicar Really, Mrs Evans—you must think what you are saying.

Meredith rises; the murmurs die down

Meredith Look here, Vicar. I wasn't here last time . . .

Mrs Preece Hereford Races.

Meredith So I'm a disinterested party as you might say . . .

Griffiths (*sitting*) Except that you've got the contract for the job.

Meredith (*loftily ignoring the interruptions*) And I propose that Mr Griffiths finishes reading the minutes and then we'll see what happens.

Miss Jones I second that. You always say the sensible thing, Mr Meredith.

Meredith and Miss Jones smile shyly at each other

Mrs Evans Go on then. Read them, Mr Griffiths. *If* you've got the nerve.

Griffiths (*rising sulkily*) Um—er—it was agreed by a vote of five to one that the church should be redecorated throughout. It was further proposed that the work should be put out to tender, but Mr Meredith had written a note to the meeting indicating that should the proposal for the redecoration go through, he would, as a member of the P.C.C., be glad to do the work for the cost of the materials only. This generous offer was accepted and the meeting closed with prayer.

Mrs Evans It needed it!

Mrs Preece This one'll need it more.

Vicar Now. Is it your pleasure that I sign these minutes as correct?

Mrs Evans No, it is not. Mr Griffiths, you said . . .

Vicar Kindly address the Chair, Mrs Evans.

Mrs Evans Silly waste of time. Still (*with exaggerated formality*) —may I ask, through the chair, if Mr Griffiths would read that bit about the vote again.

Griffiths (*with weary patience*) It was agreed by a vote of five-to-one, that the church be redecorated throughout.

Mrs Evans (*rising and pouncing*) Throughout! What you haven't mentioned, and no doubt deliberately failed to mention, is that Mr Williams objected to the apse being painted at all.

Miss Jones That's right. He did. That was what made me wonder whether we were doing the right thing.

Vicar But the matter *was* passed, five-to-one, so I really don't see . . .

Mrs Evans You wouldn't. You come here, sweeping as clean as a bull-dozer and you don't know the characters of the people you are dealing with. Griffiths and Meredith have put their heads together to destroy the most important thing in the church and they'll do it without you lot even noticing. (*She sits angrily*)

Meredith Mr Chairman, may I ask what the devil Mrs Evans is on about? It's not as if the church was a ten-sixty-six effort, is it? About seventy years old, that's all it is—and pretty ugly at that.

Miss Jones (*primly*) It's the sort the Poet Laureate likes.

Meredith He'll like it even better when it's all blue and white.

Mrs Evans (*rising and banging the table*) It's not going to *be* all blue and white. The apse is not going to be touched.

Vicar But it's been *passed* . . .

Meredith What's so special about the apse?

Mrs Evans Special? Why, the cherubs on the ceiling, of course.

Griffiths Grubby, vulgar and sentimental.

Mrs Evans So you fiddled the minutes to get them scrubbed out. Do you know—do any of you know—who painted those cherubs?

Meredith (*genially*) Michelangelo?

Mrs Evans It was the Italian prisoners in the First World War. Out of their forgiving hearts they painted those cherubs so as we should remember them and all they suffered when they were prisoners here.

Meredith Suffered? I wouldn't have minded being a prisoner in Bowen's Cross. My grandfather had some working for him. He said they practically cried when it was all over and they had to go home.

Vicar (*almost tearfully*) Please, *please* . . .

Mrs Evans (*advancing on Meredith*) You may laugh, Morgan Meredith, you may laugh. But if you had lain under that roof there, on the scaffolding, on your back, painting away . . .

Meredith I have. Doing it all yesterday . . .

Mrs Evans Painting away at a holy picture that was to be your memorial for ever more, you wouldn't laugh to hear it's to be wiped out in white emulsion.

Vicar (*rising*) I must really insist that you both sit down. This meeting is getting out of hand.

Griffiths When was it ever *in* hand? May I ask—through the chair—what exactly Mrs Evans is proposing?

Mrs Evans That the cherubs remain as they are.

Griffiths For ever?

Mrs Evans For my time, anyway. You'll paint out those cherubs over my dead body.

Meredith Well, it's a nice thought.

Griffiths (*suddenly very polite and silky*) There is one question I'd like to ask, Vicar, if I may be so bold.

Vicar Yes, Mr Griffiths?

Griffiths Mrs Evans said it was *Italian* prisoners who painted those cherubs.

Mrs Evans I did.

Griffiths During the First World War?

Mrs Evans That's right.

Griffiths But Vicar, the Italians were on *our* side in the First World War, weren't they?

Meredith Not that they were much bloody use, mind.

Vicar Indeed yes, you may be right . . .

Meredith Oh, he'll be right. "Been to Cardiff College to get a bit of knowledge" has Mr Griffiths.

Griffiths Of course I'm right. The question is, can we place any reliance on the rest of Mrs Evans's story, since her facts are so obviously unreliable?

Mrs Evans Well, p'raps it was Austrians, then. Foreigners, anyway.

Griffiths (*acidly*) Prisoners of war usually are.

Mrs Evans (*feeling she is losing ground*) All I'm saying is that Mr Williams and I do not agree to painting out the cherubs and Mr Griffiths is falsifying his minutes to make out that there was no objection at all.

Vicar Very well, Mrs Evans. You have made your point. The best thing now is to vote again, on whether the cherubs should be painted out or remain.

Griffiths I propose that . . .

Mrs Evans Just a moment, Vicar. Before we vote, will you tell me where the water supply for the new vicarage is to come from?

Vicar I really don't see . . .

Mrs Evans Where is it to come from?

All heads turn expectantly towards the Vicar

Vicar Why—the usual source, I suppose.

Mrs Evans And what is the usual source?

The Vicar's jaw drops as he stares at her

Vicar But Mrs Evans—you couldn't—you wouldn't—I don't think you're allowed . . .

Mrs Evans There comes a point, Vicar, when we must consider whether our supply might not be under too much pressure. And at the moment the pressure is very high indeed.

Vicar (*half rising*) But Mrs Evans, this is a very difficult area for water. Yours is the only source till the mains water is brought out from the town.

Meredith By which time, Vicar, you will have died from exhaustion, carrying buckets of water across two fields and the motorway.

Mrs Evans That's all I have to say. Keep the cherubs or lose your water supply. Vote away.

Vicar (*in panic*) Perhaps we should postpone the decision until the next meeting.

Meredith Oh, come on, Vicar. My scaffolding is needed at Talybont next week. I can't go putting it up and taking it down as if it was an umbrella.

Vicar I—well—I really don't know what to say.

Mrs Preece I've changed my mind. After hearing what Mrs Evans has to say about those prisoners, I think the cherubs ought to stay.

Griffiths (*groaning*) Women!

Vicar I think this would perhaps be a good time to have our usual little break and let our feelings cool down. Miss Jones, would you see whether Mrs Smith has the tea ready?

Miss Jones goes out by the door above the table

Mrs Evans Very crafty is that, Vicar, but if you think you are going to have a word on the sly with Miss Jones or Mrs Preece, you can resign yourselves to failure; I shall be at your side if you drink tea till you burst.

Mrs Preece Oh, come on, Mrs Evans. Don't get so worked up. I've come over to your side. Not that I really fancy the cherubs, mind, but to think of those poor prisoners . . .

Miss Jones pops her head in

Miss Jones Tea ready, Vicar.

Everybody files out above the table, except Meredith and Griffiths

Meredith and Griffiths move over to the window

Meredith I'm damned if I'm going to drink tea with that old fishwife!

Griffiths Nor me.

Meredith (*holding out his hip-flask*) Here. Take a nip of that. We've some thinking to do. (*He opens the window and shouts*) Owen! Get off that bloody ladder and come here quick.

Meredith shuts the window and returns to his seat; Griffiths hands him back the flask and he takes a swig

Ah. That helps to take the taste of Mrs Evans away. A proper pickle she's landed me in.

Griffiths How's that?

Meredith I've already painted out three-and-a-half cherubs.

Griffiths What? Can't you clean them up?

Meredith Not in the state the ceiling's in. All the plaster would come off with them.

Owen enters. His face has a good deal of blue paint on it

Owen I came as quick as I could, Mr Meredith. I had to clean myself up a bit first.

Griffiths Without much success.

Meredith D'ye think you could get a cup of tea for Owen, Mr Griffiths, and see how things are going out there? I don't want any fast ones pulled on me.

Griffiths See what I can do.

Griffiths goes out above the table

Meredith (*sitting; heavily*) I've bad news for you, Owen. We're not going to be allowed to paint the apse.

Owen The what?

Meredith The round bit at the end, with the cherubs on the ceiling.

Owen (*desolate*) Not paint it? Oh, Mr Meredith, you promised me I could go up on the scaffolding for that. I've been looking forward to it.

Meredith Well, I'm sorry, Owen. I reckon you've been coming on a treat lately.

Owen I know I'm a bit clumsy, Mr Meredith. Even my mam says

I've got two left hands. But I'd be ever so careful—if only I got
the chance.

Meredith Well, I don't want to disappoint you . . . (*With feigned
sudden inspirat on*). Tell you what—suppose you go up there
now, very, very careful, and do a little job for me.

Owen (*eagerly*) What sort of a job, Mr Meredith?

Meredith On the top staging, right up underneath the roof, there's
some poles I didn't need. They're up at the far end, out of the
way. Now, you go up to the top——

Owen (*ecstatically*) Up to the top . . .

Meredith —and shift those poles forward to the end near the
ladder, so we can get them down easy tomorrow, when we
start dismantling.   •

Griffiths enters with a cup of tea

Griffiths Only half a cup left.

Meredith Never mind. I'll top it up. (*He does so, from his flask*).
Think you can do that for me, Owen? There's your tea.

Owen 'Course I can, Mr Meredith. (*He drinks*) Jaweh! There's
good tea, Mrs Smith makes for the Vicar. It's a wonder he
don't look more perky with that inside him. (*He tosses off the
rest*)

Meredith Off you go, then, Owen.

Owen goes left

What's the score in the tea-room?

Griffiths Still arguing the toss. But I can see the Vicar's thinking
about his water supply. What are we going to do? We've got
to defeat that old bitch.

Meredith Oh, I've given up that battle. I know when I'm beat.

Griffiths Come on, man. It's not like you not to fight—especially
an old battle-axe like Mrs Evans.

Meredith I don't fight with battle-axes unless I've a battle-axe of
my own. I use a more delicate instrument.

Griffiths What?

Meredith Craft. (*A significant pause*) I'm sending Owen up the
scaffolding.

Griffiths You're taking a hell of a risk, aren't you?

Meredith Don't think so. Owen is all right as long as you *warn* him about things. It's the unexpected that takes him by surprise. He knows he's got to be careful going up and coming down. He won't fall off.

Griffiths So what's the point?

The rest of the Committee enter and take their places, chattering quietly

Meredith Time will tell, man, time will tell.

Vicar Well, ladies and gentlemen: in the light of somewhat changed circumstances we must consider the problem of the— er—the cherubs.

Mrs Preece As I said, I've come round to Mrs Evans's view. I'm for keeping them. For sentimental reasons.

Vicar Miss Jones?

Miss Jones I'm sorry, Mrs Evans, but I think we should paint the whole church. I'm sad for the cherubs, mind, but they *are* a bit old-fashioned.

Mrs Evans You'll be saying the Bible's old-fashioned next. And of course you would side with Morgan Meredith.

Miss Jones (*startled*) I don't know why you should say that, Mrs Evans.

Vicar (*hastily*) Mr Griffiths?

Griffiths Get rid of the shabby things. If we keep them it makes nonsense of the redecorating that's already been done.

Vicar Mr Meredith?

Mrs Evans No need to ask *him*. He's an interested party. And if you think he's doing this out of the kindness of his heart and is making no profit, then you're as simple as you look—and that's saying something.

Meredith (*rising in great dignity*) I am sorry Mrs Evans should think of me in this way. In the light of what she has implied, I prefer not to vote, Vicar. (*He crosses to the window and looks out*)

Vicar But that means . . . (*He looks wildly round*)

Mrs Evans Two for the cherubs and two against. You'll have to give the casting vote, Vicar.

Vicar Mr Meredith, PLEASE!

Meredith (*nobly*) No, Vicar. I shall not vote. Mrs Evans's words have cut too deep.

Mrs Evans I hope you'll enjoy carrying every drop of water across those fields, Vicar.

Vicar Oh dear, oh dear! I don't know what to say. It's blackmail, Mrs Evans. I don't think legally you can . . .

Griffiths Ah, you may have a point there, Vicar. I should say that the Evanses have a contract to supply the village with water . . .

Mrs Evans (*hastily*) Nothing in writing, nothing in writing.

Griffiths And that if they don't fulfil that contract the Local Authority might take over the supply.

Mrs Evans First I've heard of it!

Meredith There's none so deaf as those who won't hear.

Mrs Evans I hear things about *you*, Morgan Meredith, as are causing comment in the village. And you a respectable widower of ten years' standing.

Meredith And what is wrong about being a widower?

Mrs Evans Always at the school-house. Hanging around . . .

Miss Jones reacts sharply

Meredith I wasn't hanging around. I was hanging pictures. For Miss Jones.

Mrs Evans Miss Jones must have a lot of pictures. Three evenings last week you were hanging them.

Miss Jones (*rising, distressed and bewildered*) Mrs Evans! What are you implying?

Vicar Ladies! LADIES!

Griffiths Here we go. (*He picks up his pen and writes down all that is said with rapidity*).

Miss Jones I'm sorry, Vicar, but my reputation is at stake.

Mrs Evans Huh! What's left of it!

Miss Jones (*near tears*) Mr Meredith very kindly put up some pictures for me because the walls are difficult—very difficult.

Mrs Evans (*with venomous sweetness*) As difficult as the situation you find yourself in?

Meredith What situation? You can't knock a nail in without plaster falling out like dandruff. I had to go back a second time to fill in the holes.

Miss Jones As for the third evening Mr Meredith came round . . .

Meredith Don't you make excuses to Mrs Evans, my dear. You're an independent, good-living young woman, which is more than can be said of some I could mention.

Mrs Evans Is it my fault if I hear comments passed in the post office, where I happened to be renewing my television licence, which is more than can be said of some *I* could mention.

Miss Jones (*faintly*) The post office?

Meredith Good God! You might as well broadcast it on telly as in the post office.

Miss Jones But what did they *say*?

Mrs Evans They said that you, Morgan Meredith, were after Miss Jones.

Miss Jones (*bursting into tears*) Oh! Oh!

Mrs Evans But they added that you'd never hang up your hat in her hall for good, because you never paid cash for anything if you could get it on tick!

Miss Jones Oh, the lies—the humiliation! (*Moving to Meredith*) Mr Meredith, I am sorry if I have caused you any embarrassment . . . (*She is overcome by sobs*) It's dreadful, dreadful—you must excuse me, Vicar. I'm so upset . . . (*She makes for the door above the window*)

Meredith slams his hand down on the table

Meredith Gwyneth Jones!

Miss Jones looks round, startled

You stay where you are a minute

Miss Jones is so startled she stops crying

(*Leaning threateningly across the table to Mrs Evans*) So they said that, did they? Not that I believe a word of it. It's your own bloody-mindedness that makes you think of such things.

Mrs Evans half rises

Listen to me, woman!

Mrs Evans sinks back. The Vicar buries his face in his hands

(*To Miss Jones*) And you listen to. (*He goes to her*) Gwyneth Jones, will you marry me?

Mrs Preece (*ecstatically*) Oh, there's lovely!

Griffiths (*urgently*) My pen's run out! Lend me one, someone. (*He picks a pen from the Vicar's breast pocket and continues to scribble*).

Vicar (*desperately*) This is a P.C.C. meeting!

Meredith And you're chairman of it. So listen. Now Gwyneth Jones. (*He pulls her forward quite roughly*) Answer in front of the Vicar. Will you have me? Yes, or no?

Miss Jones (*after a few seconds of stunned bewilderment, pulling herself together and becoming the schoolmistress again*). And who do you think you are, Morgan Meredith, to speak to me like that? In front of everyone, too. That is not the way to behave. Not nice at all. You'll stay behind after school—I mean after the meeting, and I'll give you a piece of my mind.

Miss Jones goes out through the door right

Mrs Evans (*laughing*) That's cut *you* down to size, Morgan Meredith.

Meredith (*flinging himself back into his chair*) All right! All right! Go back to the post office and tell everyone that Miss Jones jilted me in public.

Vicar PLEASE may we . . .

Owen's voice is heard off

Owen (*off*) Mr Meredith, Mr Meredith!

Meredith goes to the window

Mrs Preece Listen! That's Owen Pugh.

Owen Help, help!

Griffiths (*rising*) Sounds as if he's in trouble.

Meredith (*turning, grinning, from window*) Good old Owen.

Owen bursts in, his hair full of plaster, his face and clothes covered in dust

Meredith You all right, Owen?

Owen (*breathless*) I am, sir, but oh, sir . . .

Vicar (*concerned, giving Owen a chair*) Here, sit down, boy.

Everyone gathers round

Griffiths Have you had an accident, lad?

Mrs Preece Oh, Owen, Owen. You always were cack-handed. What is it now?

Vicar Have you been up on the scaffolding, Owen?

Owen Mr Meredith did give me permission, sir. He asked me to shift the spare poles forward for him. Before we started dismantling the scaffolding.

Mrs Evans Dismantling?

Meredith Oh, I know when I'm beaten, Mrs Evans.

Mrs Evans inhales with triumph

When I saw you'd got the upper hand, I told Owen to start the demolition work.

Owen (*miserably*) You used the right word there, Mr Meredith.

Meredith What word, boy?

Owen Demolition. I forgot I was so near the roof, see. (*Rising and illustrating*) I lifted up one of those long bars at the back and tried to turn round sideways-like—and it was that long there wasn't room. So I up-ended it—(*he mimes*)—so—(*he looks upward and ducks from an imaginary shower of plaster; apologetically*) It hit the ceiling a hell of a wham, Mr Meredith.

Vicar (*gibbering*) The ceiling? Where? Where?

Owen Bang in the middle of a cherub.

Mrs Evans screams and has to sit

Meredith Damage it much, boy?

Owen I don't know what you call much, Mr Meredith; but there's a ruddy great hole in the plaster and cracks down into the ten commandments.

Mrs Evans It's a plot! A wicked plot!

Vicar (*in anguish*) Cracks! How far down, Owen?

Owen "Honour thy father and mother" on one side and "adultery" on the other.

Griffiths (*amused at last*) In fact there's been nothing like it since Moses dropped the original tablets.

Mrs Evans Blasphemy! Blasphemy on top of sacrilege! And you a church-warden!

Griffiths Those cherubs must have been holding up the ceiling with their wing-tips. If we'd listened to Mrs Evans we might have had a parish tragedy.

Meredith Nasty advert for the church that might've been. Can't
you see the headlines? "Falling cherubs strike down Vicar
during Family Service!"

Mrs Evans (*beside herself*) Oh, I wish they had, I wish they had!
If ever I saw a hand-picked put-up job, Morgan Meredith, it's
this one.

Meredith (*with wounded innocence*) Put-up? And I sitting arguing
with you at the time?

Mrs Preece And Owen, poor boy, in danger of his life. I've
changed my mind again, Vicar. After this, the cherubs must go.

Owen (*mournfully*) Don't worry. They've gone.

Mrs Evans (*sweeping to door and turning*) And I'm going too.
This P.C.C. stinks of corruption. There's you, Griffiths, falsifying your minutes; there's Morgan Meredith about as straight
as a corkscrew; there's that schoolmistress no better than she
should be, and as for you, Vicar, you are nothing but a whited
sepulchre in sheep's clothing. Words fail me!

Mrs Evans sweeps out, banging the door left

Meredith Words fail her! No such luck.

Griffiths (*rubbing his hands with satisfaction*) Well, well, Mr
Chairman. I think this is the moment when you ask if there's
any other business.

The Vicar begins gathering his papers together distractedly

Mrs Preece Oh, there is. The date of the fête, the Sunday School
Outing, the Mothers' Union Outing . . .

Vicar (*agitatedly*) It must wait, it must wait. I must get over to
the church and see the damage. Any other business, no, then
the meeting is closed. Come with me please, Mr Griffiths.

The Vicar and Griffiths go

Mrs Preece Well! Didn't even close with prayer! Coming to see
the damage, Mr Meredith?

Meredith I'll be seeing it soon enough.

Mrs Preece 'Bye for now, then!

Mrs Preece goes

Meredith Go and get cleaned up, boy.

Owen turns to go

And on your way through, tell Miss Jones I've stayed behind, like she said.

Owen Stay behind? You in trouble, Mr Meredith?

Meredith She's angry with me, Owen. Told me to stay behind and she'd give me a piece of her mind.

Owen Oh, that don't mean nothing, Mr Meredith. She often used to say that to me in school. And then she'd give me a sweetie and tell me to run off home.

Meredith (*brightening*) Did she, now?

Owen That's what a piece of her mind is, I'm thinking. A sweetie.

Meredith I hope you're right, boy. Anyway, tell her I'm here.

Owen goes right

Meredith takes up a naughty-schoolboy stance, facing the audience, hands behind him, face down

Miss Jones enters

Miss Jones (*severely*) So there you are, Morgan Meredith. What have you got to say for yourself?

Meredith (*mumbling*) Nothing, Miss Jones.

Miss Jones Nothing?

Meredith I'm sorry, Miss Jones.

Miss Jones That's better. You know you behaved badly, don't you?

Meredith Yes, Miss Jones. (*He raises his head and adds less meekly*) But I was provoked.

Miss Jones Well, I'll overlook it this time. Words spoken in anger are best forgotten.

Meredith (*bluntly; himself again*) But I don't want you to forget. I meant what I said. Will you marry me?

Miss Jones (*considering; turning away*) That depends. There are some things I like about you, Morgan. Many things. (*Turning*) But sometimes you are a bit too—smart. Too clever by half. In business—you know—cutting corners—taking advantage . . . Not always quite straight.

Meredith Oh.

Miss Jones That would have to stop. Straight dealing or nothing.

Meredith I see.

Miss Jones Think it over. And so will I.

Meredith (*brightening*) Can I come and see you when I've thought?

Miss Jones Well now . . . (*She pauses, considering. Then, with a glint of mischief*) You know my grandfather clock in the hall? It's stopped. I think p'raps it's not standing level.

Meredith (*with alacrity*) Don't worry, Gwyneth, don't worry. I'll be round this evening.

Miss Jones (*smiling*) This evening, then.

He attempts an embrace, but she ducks away and raps him gently

This evening, I said. Good-bye for now.

Miss Jones goes left

Meredith (*looking at the thermometer*) Not a bad afternoon's work. Mrs Evans out. Miss Jones in. Repair bill up. (*He screws his eyes up in calculation*) To filling and making good holes in ceiling . . . (*He moves the thermometer up to three thousand five hundred*) To repairing the ten commandments . . . (*He moves it up still farther*) Not a bad afternoon's work at all. (*He comes forward, taking out his pipe*)

Owen looks in at the door, rubbing his face with a towel

Owen Did she give you a sweetie, Mr Meredith?

Meredith Well—(*smiling to himself*)—I think she did, boy. (*He puts his pipe in his mouth and feels for matches, then removes the pipe to add*) Or if she didn't—(*he strikes a match*)—she will!

Meredith bends to light his pipe, as—

the CURTAIN *falls quickly*

FURNITURE AND PROPERTY LIST

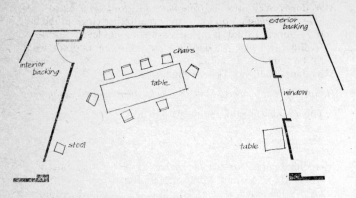

On stage: Long baize-covered table. *On it:* papers, pencils
Small table. *On it:* carafe of water, glass
8 small chairs
Stool
On wall: notice-board with various notices
Off stage: Large cardboard cut-out thermometer **(Owen, Gareth)**
Blue paint **(Owen)**
Cup of tea **(Griffiths)**
Plaster and dust **(Owen)**
Towel **(Owen)**
Personal: **Griffiths:** watch, 2 opened letters, pen
Meredith: hip-flask, pipe, matches
Vicar: pen